I want to
know about the
Bible

Christina Goodings

Illustrated by
Jan Lewis

LION
CHILDREN'S

Contents

1 Stories of the Beginning

2 Noah and the Flood

3 Abraham and the Blessing

4 Slaves in Egypt

5 Moses and the Covenant

6 A Land to Call Home

7 Jerusalem

8 Israel and its Prophets

9 Judah and its Prophets

10 A Faraway Land

11 The Persian Empire

12 The Homecoming

13 Waiting for a King

14 Mark and the Story of Jesus

15 Matthew and the Story of Jesus

16 Luke and the Story of Jesus

17 John and the Story of Jesus

18 The First Christians

19 Letters to Christians

20 Gathering the Books

Index

1 Stories of the Beginning

STORIES TOLD ALOUD

The first stories in the Bible are the ancient tales of the Jewish people. From thousands of years ago, they were told by grown-ups to their children. In this way, they were treasured long before they were written down.

The first story in the Bible is about the making of the world.

In the beginning, it says, there was nothing. God spoke to the emptiness: 'Let there be light.' The light shone, and it was very, very good. That was the first day.

On the next day, God spoke again. Yet more things came into being. At the end of six days, the world and everything in it was made, and it was all very, very good.

On the seventh day, God rested.

Children learn the traditional tales from a storyteller

The second story is about the first man and the first woman.

God planted a garden. It was a paradise home for Adam and Eve, and its trees and plants gave them all they needed. There they lived in peace with the other creatures.

There was one thing they must not do: eat from a forbidden tree. Its fruit was like poison and would let evil things into their world.

But a snake came and whispered to Eve that God had lied: the fruit would only make them wise.

Eve ate, and then Adam. At once they knew their world was ruined. They had to leave their paradise home and go out into a world where good things and bad things were mixed together.

THE BOOK OF BOOKS

The Christian Bible looks like just one book. In fact, it is a collection of over sixty books. The oldest are the holy books of the Jewish people and tell the history of their ancestors, the people of Israel. The newer ones are about Jesus and his followers.

*Each book has a different name. The first is **Genesis**. This word means 'birth' or 'beginning'. Genesis contains stories about the beginning of everything.*

The story of Adam and Eve explains why the world is a mixture of good and bad

2 Noah and the Flood

BOOK, CHAPTER AND VERSE

To look up a story in the Bible, it is helpful to know its three-part 'address'.

The first part of the address is the name of the book. These names are very ancient.

The other two parts are more recent, but still hundreds of years old. Each book is divided into numbered chapters. Each chapter is divided into numbered verses.

*The story of Noah begins in the first book of the Bible, **Genesis**, chapter 6, verse 9.*

One of the best-known stories in the Bible is about Noah. It tells of a promise God made.

God had made a good world; but people chose to go their own way. They began to quarrel and to fight and to do all kinds of evil things. In the end, there was only one good man: Noah.

God spoke to Noah: 'I have decided to put an end to all this wickedness. First, I want you to build a boat: big enough for you, your family and a mother and a father of every kind of living creature. Take on board enough food to last all of you for many days.'

Noah obeyed. When everyone was safe on board, God sent rain. Day after day it rained. Soon flood water covered all the world.

The story of the great flood is about God wanting to wash away all that is bad

The rainbow becomes a
sign of God's love
and care

Animals set off to find
homes and have families

Days and weeks went by. The rain stopped; the
boat crunched to a stop. But there was still water
all around. One day, Noah sent out a dove. It
returned with a fresh olive leaf in its beak. It was
a hopeful sign.

Slowly, slowly the water ebbed away. God spoke
to Noah: 'It is time for all of you to leave the boat.
It is time to fill the world with new life again.'

Noah did so. He and his family held a
thanksgiving party. As they did, God put a rainbow
in the sky. 'It is a sign of my promise,' said God.
'Never again will I flood the world. There will
always be summer and winter, seedtime and
harvest.'

3 Abraham and the Blessing

The Bible contains many books, but together they tell one great story. It is the story of God and God's people.

According to the Bible, the father of God's people is a man named Abraham. He lived in Babylonia, but one day God told him that he must find a new home.

'Go to a land I will show to you,' said God, 'the land of Canaan. There, you will have children and grandchildren, and they will become a nation. I will bless you and your people; through them, I will bless everyone in the world.'

Abraham had great faith in God, and he set out. With him he took his wife Sarah, his nephew Lot, all their servants and flocks of sheep, goats and cattle. For many years they lived as nomads, setting up camp when they found good pasture and then moving on to find new pastures. The years went by, but still Abraham and Sarah had no children. In fact, Sarah was sure she had grown too old ever to have a child.

Then came good news: she was pregnant. Abraham and Sarah named their son Isaac, and he brought them joy and laughter.

Abraham looks at the night sky. God has said his family will be more than all the stars he can see

The promises God had made to Abraham were handed down to Isaac's son Jacob. God gave him a new name, Israel. His twelve sons also had families, and there were more children and yet more grandchildren. It was not long before the family to whom God had made promises were a nation: the people of Israel.

Abraham's family live in tents so they can move to find grass for their flocks of sheep

4 Slaves in Egypt

Jacob and his family lived in Canaan. They believed it was the land God had promised them. But then came an important lesson.

Jacob had a favourite son: Joseph. His ten older brothers were jealous when their father gave Joseph an expensive coat. They were angry when Joseph boasted about his dreams in which all his family bowed down to him.

To get rid of him, they sold him as a slave and told Jacob he was dead.

Joseph was taken to Egypt. Everything seemed to go wrong and he ended up in jail. But God gave him the wisdom to explain dreams. One day, he explained the meaning of a dream that was troubling the king. The dream was about a coming famine and the king promoted Joseph to a very important job: organizing the stores of food. When famine struck, Joseph's family came begging to buy food. They bowed down to the Egyptian official in charge: they did not know it was their brother.

Joseph's wonderful coat shows he is the favourite son

Joseph checks that extra grain is stored for the years of bad harvests

Joseph recognized them and wept. He wanted to see his father and younger brother Benjamin again. In the end, he forgave them all and invited them to come and live in Egypt. There they prospered.

Hundreds of years went by. The people of Israel grew to be a big nation. The new king of Egypt was unhappy about having so many foreigners in his land. He decided to make them his slaves.

Then the Israelites knew what it was like to be poor. They knew what it was like to have no rights. They knew what it was like to have no one to help them.

THE LESSON OF EGYPT

The Israelites never forgot the time their people were slaves. The Bible is full of reminders like this one:

'Do not ill-treat foreigners who are living in your land. Treat them as you would a fellow-Israelite, and love them as you love yourselves.'

5 Moses and the Covenant

Princess

Miriam

Baby Moses

Tall papyrus hides the baby in the basket

COVENANT

Another word for covenant is 'testament'. The older books of the Bible are about the people of Israel and God's covenant with them. Christians call these books the Old Testament.

The king of Egypt treated the Israelites more and more cruelly. He ordered all their baby boys to be thrown in the river. One mother hid her baby in a floating cradle. His name was Moses. An Egyptian princess found him and kept him safe.

As a young man, Moses was angry to see his own people suffering. One day, he believed he heard God calling him to lead his people to freedom.

The king would not agree. Disasters came, but the king did not believe Moses when he said these were warnings from God. Then, one dark night, the firstborn son in every Egyptian home died. Only the Israelites were spared. The king of Egypt grew frightened and let the people go free. Even though he later chased after them, God kept them safe.

For ever after, the people of Israel had a festival to remember when death passed them by: Passover.

The Israelites spent many years in the wild country between Egypt and Canaan. On the way, Moses gave them laws. Some laws were about how to worship God. Others were about how to treat one another in a way that was kind and fair.

These laws were part of an agreement, or covenant, with God: if they obeyed them, God would be their God and they would be God's people. The great laws were written down and kept in a golden box – the ark of the covenant – in their place of worship: a special tent called the tabernacle.

Moses

The Ten Commandments are written in stone – a sign they should last for ever

THE BOOKS OF MOSES

*The first five books of the Bible are sometimes called the books of Moses and sometimes the books of the Law. **Genesis** is about the beginnings of the people of Israel. **Exodus** means 'coming out' and is about the escape from Egypt. This book, along with **Leviticus**, **Numbers** and **Deuteronomy**, contains many laws that Moses is said to have taught the people. Among them were two great commandments:*

'Love the Lord your God with all your heart, with all your soul, and with all your strength.'

'Love your neighbour as you love yourself.'

6 A Land to Call Home

Joshua

Priests

By a miracle, the walls of Jericho fall down

JOSHUA AND THE LAW

At the beginning of the story of Joshua, the Bible tells what God said to the young leader:

'Be sure that the book of the Law is always read in your worship. Study it day and night, and make sure that you obey everything written in it. Then you will be prosperous and successful.'

The great leader Moses grew old. He chose a brave young soldier named Joshua to lead the people of Israel to their new home in Canaan.

The Bible book called **Joshua** says that the young leader's first victory was over the Canaanite city of Jericho. Its walls were high and its gates were strong, but God told Joshua what to do. Once a day, for six days, Joshua led a procession around the city. On the seventh day, the procession went round seven times. Joshua gave a signal: the priests blew trumpets, the people shouted aloud – and by a miracle, the city walls fell down.

Joshua went on to many victories and gave each of the great families of Israel a share of the land of Canaan.

Years went by, and life was often hard. The people of Israel found it hard to trust in their God. They began to worship the gods of the Canaanites as well. That only made things worse. Enemy nations all around attacked them and robbed them.

The Bible book called **Judges** tells astonishing tales of the heroes God chose to defend the people and bring justice. Some of the stories are violent, but the message is clear: those who are faithful to God will be safe in the land; those who are unfaithful will be defeated.

The last of the judges was a man who listened to God – a prophet. His name was Samuel. The book called **1 Samuel** tells of how, as a young helper in the place of worship, he heard God calling him. He grew up to be a wise leader, helping his people to worship God and to live in peace with one another.

The hero named Samson has amazing strength

RUTH

The very short book of **Ruth** is set in the time of the judges. It is a happy story of how an Israelite community welcomes a foreigner and takes care of her.

Samuel hears God speaking to him

7 Jerusalem

Goliath

David wins
a battle because
he trusts in God

The prophet Samuel grew old, and the people asked him to choose their next leader. But they were tired of enemy attacks. Now they wanted a king.

With God's help, Samuel chose a strong and handsome man named Saul. He gathered an army and won many battles. But the enemies called Philistines could not easily be beaten. One day, their champion warrior, Goliath, challenged the people of Israel to a one-against-one fight that would decide the war.

The Bible tells the story of a shepherd boy from Bethlehem who came to the rescue. His name was David, and he believed God would help him win. Goliath had sharp weapons and gleaming armour, but David knocked him down with a well-aimed stone from his sling.

PSALMS AND THE BOOKS OF WISDOM

*Special songs, the **Psalms**, were written to be used in Temple worship. Some may have been written by David, who was admired as a musician from the time he was a shepherd boy.*

*When Solomon became king, says the Bible, he asked God for wisdom. There is a collection of wise sayings in the Bible, known as **Proverbs**, that are said to be the work of Solomon.*

*Another book said to be by Solomon is a love poem called the **Song of Songs**. Other so-called books of wisdom are **Ecclesiastes** and **Job**.*

David's victory made him a hero and, when Saul died, he became the next king. He defeated all the nation's rivals. He decided to build a capital city: Jerusalem.

It was in Jerusalem that the next king, David's son, Solomon, built a Temple for God to replace the ancient tabernacle. The treasured ark of the covenant was placed in its inner room.

WRITING THE BIBLE

There was time for learning in Solomon's wealthy kingdom. It was probably at this time that the ancient stories of the people first began to be collected and treasured in written form.

King Solomon

Priests

Ark of the covenant

8 Israel and its Prophets

Jezebel

King Ahab

THE NATION'S HISTORY

The history of the kings and the kingdoms of Israel and Judah can be found in the Bible books called **1 Samuel**, **2 Samuel**, **1 Kings** *and* **2 Kings**. *The same stories also appear in two history books that were written later:* **1 Chronicles** *and* **2 Chronicles**.

When King Solomon died, the areas to the north wanted to be free and to choose their own king. They called their kingdom Israel. The area around Jerusalem stayed loyal to Solomon's son. Their little kingdom was Judah.

The first king in the north was Jeroboam. He wanted his people to live as God's people and keep God's laws. However, the kings who came after him did not have the same ideas. One of them, King Ahab, married a foreign princess named Jezebel and encouraged his people to worship her gods. He also allowed her to go ahead with one very nasty plan.

Ahab had seen a vineyard and thought it would make a nice garden. However, God's laws did not permit him to buy land from someone else's family. Jezebel found out that the owner was Naboth. She arranged for him to be accused of a crime he didn't commit and put to death. Then she told Ahab the land was his.

Time and again God sent the prophet Elijah to warn Ahab about his wrongdoing, but the arrogant king would not change his ways. The result was a horrible death.

The years went by and God sent other prophets, including Elisha, Hosea and Amos. But the nation

Elijah shows how powerful God is by calling down fire from heaven

Ahab is terrified of Elijah's God

did not care about living as God's people. In the end, they were destroyed by the armies of Assyria. By 722 BCE the kingdom was no more and the people had been sent to live in other parts of the Assyrian empire.

9 Judah and its Prophets

Josiah reads the book of the Law

A COLLECTION OF WRITINGS

During the reign of King Josiah, scholars began to pay attention to all the important books written about the nation. The followers of the prophets began to write down the prophets' teachings. More books that eventually became part of the Bible were begun in this way.

In the kingdom of Judah, as in the northern kingdom of Israel, kings and people failed to live up to God's standards. However, they were shaken when the kingdom of Israel was destroyed by the armies of Assyria. The disaster made the Judeans listen to the warnings of their prophets, including Isaiah and Micah. Isaiah advised King Hezekiah of Judah what to do when the Assyrian army came and camped outside Jerusalem. Together they trusted God to keep the city safe. One night, thousands of Assyrian soldiers died and the army went away without attacking.

Some time later, around 622 BCE, an ancient book of the Law was found in the Temple in Jerusalem. The king, Josiah, was dismayed to learn how much it had been ignored. He gave orders for the Temple to be put to rights and for the people to remember all that it meant to live as God's people.

Even so, there was trouble ahead for Judah. Rival nations were fighting for power: Egypt to the south, Assyria to the north and, east of Assyria, another superpower: Babylon.

The kings who came after Josiah did not listen to

*The books of the prophets **Isaiah** and **Micah** deal with the time when Judah was threatened by Assyria. The book of the prophet **Nahum** gives thanks for the defeat of the Assyrians by the armies of Babylon.*

*However, those same armies eventually threatened Judah. **Jeremiah**, **Zephaniah** and **Habakkuk** warned the kings of Judah about the threat.*

*A poem called **Lamentations** describes the horror of Jerusalem after the defeat, and the prophet **Obadiah** predicted disaster for the Edomites who came looting.*

the advice of their prophets. In the end, the armies of Babylon attacked Jerusalem. They burned the Temple. The precious ark of the covenant went missing and has never been found.

The ruined city of Jerusalem is a place where owls hoot and jackals roam

10 A Faraway Land

The Babylonians not only defeated Judah; they also took many of its most talented people to their capital city, Babylon. The people of Judah no longer felt like a nation. What could they do to live as God's people – God's holy nation?

They began to treasure all the writings that might help – the books of the Law and the words of the prophets. They knew that one of their great laws told them to respect the weekly day of rest – the sabbath – and they began to meet on this day to study the writings. In them they discovered other things they could do to show their respect for God – observing the festival, obeying the laws about which foods to eat and how to prepare them.

It was at this time that the people from Judah became known as Jews. Their weekly meeting led to the building of meeting places – synagogues. They became known for their habit of saying prayers, keeping special festivals and having special customs.

All these things set them apart from other people in the empire, and they were not always popular.

Far from home, Jewish people praise God and study the Law

The Bible book of **Daniel** included stories to encourage them.

One story was of three Jewish men who refused to bow down to the statue of the Babylonian god. The king punished them by throwing them into a fiery furnace. He was dismayed to see a fourth figure walking around in the flames: their God had sent an angel to protect them. He ordered them to be set free.

Angel

Shadrach

Meshach

Abednego

The story of three men in the fiery furnace is about God taking care of those who are faithful

11 The Persian Empire

In 539 BCE, the armies of Persia defeated the armies of Babylon. Two famous Bible stories are set in the Persian empire.

One is in the book of **Daniel**. It tells of a Jewish exile named Daniel, who served the king of Babylon and who predicted Babylon's defeat. The new Persian king found that Daniel was trustworthy and he gave him a very important job in his government.

That made other officials jealous. Enemies plotted against him and tricked the king into making a law that Daniel was bound to break: it got him into trouble simply for saying his prayers.

It was the king's new law, so even the king could not save him from the punishment. Daniel was thrown into a pit of hungry lions.

But God knew that Daniel had done no wrong and did not

Daniel trusts in God

26

Queen Esther

King

Cruel
Haman

deserve to die. Instead, God sent an angel to keep him safe in the pit all through a long, dark night. In the morning, the king was very pleased to be able to set Daniel free.

Another story is told in the book of **Esther**. Esther was a very beautiful Jewish woman and she became the king's favourite wife. However, one of the palace advisors – a man named Haman – hated the Jewish people. He persuaded the king that they were disloyal and should be killed. In the royal court, Esther did not have any real power. She knew that it was her place as a wife to wait for the king to summon her; she risked severe punishment if she went to him uninvited. However, bravely she went and asked him for a favour. She pleaded for him to save her people. Haman was put to death for his wickedness and the Jewish people were saved.

JOEL

*In the Bible is the book of the prophet **Joel**. It seems to belong to the time of the Persian empire and it pleads with the people to be faithful to God, even when everything seems to be going wrong:*

*   'Come back to the Lord your God.*
*   He is kind and full of mercy;*
*   he is patient and keeps his promise;*
*   he is always ready to forgive and not punish.'*

12 The Homecoming

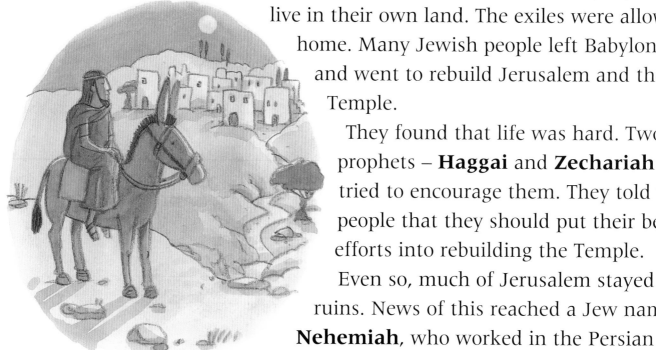

The Persian rulers were happy to let people go to live in their own land. The exiles were allowed home. Many Jewish people left Babylon and went to rebuild Jerusalem and the Temple.

They found that life was hard. Two prophets – **Haggai** and **Zechariah** – tried to encourage them. They told the people that they should put their best efforts into rebuilding the Temple.

Even so, much of Jerusalem stayed in ruins. News of this reached a Jew named **Nehemiah**, who worked in the Persian royal palace. He asked for permission to go to help rebuild the city. There, he encouraged everyone to complete the rebuilding, including strong city walls.

Other people worked hard to remind everyone of God's standards. One was a prophet named **Malachi** and another a priest named **Ezra**. Ezra made sure that the Law was read aloud and he encouraged everyone to obey it.

Ezra wanted the Jewish people to obey the Law and keep their own traditions. He didn't want them to have anything to do with foreigners. The story of **Jonah** gives a different view.

Nehemiah is sad as he looks at Jerusalem

THE JEWISH SCRIPTURES

In the time of Ezra, Jewish scholars took a fresh look at the collection of all their precious writings, old and new. These were treasured as the books of their faith – their scriptures.

Jonah was a prophet. God told him to go to preach to the Assyrians in Nineveh and tell them to change their wicked ways. Jonah did not want to help the foreigners, so he got on a boat to sail far away.

Then came a storm. Jonah realized that God wasn't going to let him escape, so he asked the sailors to throw him into the sea.

A big fish swallowed Jonah and took him to land. Jonah went and preached in Nineveh. To Jonah's astonishment, the Ninevites changed their wicked ways – and God forgave them.

What kind of sea creature could swallow a man?

Jonah

13 Waiting for a King

The Persian empire did not last for ever. First, the Greeks led by Alexander the Great conquered many lands. The people of Jerusalem were forced to allow statues of Greek gods in their Temple and only managed to get rid of them and put it to rights after a fierce struggle.

Many years after that, the Romans became the most powerful people in the world. The land of the Jews was ruled by the emperor in Rome and everyone had to pay him taxes.

The Romans chose a man named Herod to be king in Jerusalem. He did something spectacular to make sure that both Jews and Romans admired him: he arranged for a splendid new Temple to be built.

Even so, the Jewish people still remembered the old days: the time when King David had fought for their freedom and made them respected. They read the words of the prophets, who promised that God would never forget them… and that one day God would send a new king.

King Herod rebuilds the Temple in Jerusalem

The Hebrew word for 'chosen king' was 'messiah'. In Greek, the word was 'Christ'. They were longing for that king.

In time, a prophet named John became famous. He told people to turn away from wrongdoing and be baptized. It would be a sign that they wanted to live as God's people. John the Baptist made a very important announcement:

'The man who will come after me is much greater than I am. I am not good enough even to bend down and untie his sandals. I baptize you with water, but he will baptize you with the Holy Spirit.'

These words are found in one of the Bible books that is about Jesus: the Gospel of **Mark**, chapter 1, verses 7 and 8.

LANGUAGES

From the time of the Greek empire, Greek became the most usual language for writing books. All the Bible stories about Jesus were first written in Greek.

John the Baptist

14 Mark and the Story of Jesus

In the time of the Romans, a man named Jesus began to preach. He did most of his teaching in the region known as Galilee and caused a great stir.

Even after his death, more and more people wanted to follow Jesus' teachings and to know more about his life.

One of his followers wrote a book to help the followers of Jesus who lived in Rome: it is known as the Gospel of **Mark**.

Mark says that Jesus preached about a new kingdom.

' "The right time has come," he said, "and the kingdom of God is near! Turn away from your sins and believe the Good News!" '

People wondered what the kingdom was. Jesus gave answers, but they were often puzzling.

'The kingdom of God is like a seed,' he once said. 'When it is sown, it is tiny. After a while, it grows up and becomes a huge tree, and birds come and nest in its branches.'

Jesus gathered a loyal band of followers, or disciples, to help God's

Jesus says the kingdom of God is like a tree where birds nest

kingdom to grow. Among them were four men who had worked as fishermen on Lake Galilee: Simon, also called Peter, and his brother Andrew; James and his brother John.

The thing that made many other people pay attention to Jesus was the miracles. Everyone began to talk about how he could heal people with just a word or a touch. Some people began to wonder if he was indeed the promised messiah, the Christ.

Not everyone was impressed. The priests in the Temple and the rabbis who taught in the synagogues began to whisper about his teaching. Was he being faithful to the Law, they worried?

In the end, they plotted Jesus' death. They asked the Roman governor Pontius Pilate to order his execution. Jesus was crucified on a hill outside Jerusalem. Three days later, his friends saw him alive.

THE GOSPEL OF MARK

*The book of Mark in the Bible is called a Gospel – a word meaning 'good news'. No one knows for sure who Mark was, but he may have been the 'John Mark' mentioned in the book of **Acts**. John Mark helped spread the news about Jesus as he journeyed to different countries with a relative named Barnabas.*

Religious leaders whisper about Jesus

15 Matthew and the Story of Jesus

Matthew's Gospel tells the Nativity story of the wise men and their gifts

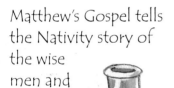

Jar of myrrh

Box of frankincense

Gold

The Gospel that **Mark** wrote seems to have inspired two others to write an account of the life of Jesus. One of these is known as the Gospel of **Matthew**. It borrows many stories from Mark – sometimes word for word – but has others as well.

Matthew seems to have been written for Jewish people who believed in Jesus. He is careful to point out that, in Jesus, promises in the Jewish scriptures are coming true.

This is true of his story of Jesus' birth. He points out that Jesus is descended from King David. Like him, as the prophet **Micah** foretold, he was born in Bethlehem.

Matthew says that some foreigners from the East were given a sign that Jesus was special. They saw a star in the night sky and believed it was telling them that a king of the Jewish people had been born. They came and found him, and gave him gifts of gold, frankincense and myrrh. Ancient prophecies had foretold that other nations would once again respect the Jews.

Matthew also tells about Jesus' teaching:

' "You have heard that it was said, 'Love your friends, hate your enemies.' But now I tell you: love your enemies and

Lake Galilee

Jesus

pray for those who persecute you, so that you may
become the children of your Father in heaven."'

Matthew also says that Jesus taught his followers
a prayer.

Like the other Gospels, Matthew tells of Jesus'
teachings and his miracles, and about the religious
leaders who plotted his death. He also makes it
clear that Jesus' followers claimed to have seen him
alive again. They said Jesus told them to spread the
news about him and win many more followers.

People are eager to hear
what Jesus says

16 Luke and the Story of Jesus

WHO WAS LUKE?

*Luke was a doctor. Because he had a good education, he told the stories well and wrote in good Greek. About half of Luke's book is based on the Gospel of **Mark**; other bits come from the same source as **Matthew** used. About a third is special to Luke.*

As the news about Jesus spread, it was not only Jews who believed the message. Non-Jews, or Gentiles, also became devoted followers. One of these was **Luke** and he helped another follower, a Jew named Paul, to spread the message to other countries in the Roman empire. He wrote a Gospel for Gentile believers.

Luke's account of the birth of Jesus tells of an angel, Gabriel, coming to visit Mary. The angel told Mary that her child would be God's Son.

Mary and her husband-to-be lived in Nazareth, in Galilee. They had to travel to Bethlehem because the Roman emperor had ordered a count of all the people who paid taxes. They had to shelter in a room with the animals. There Mary's baby was born.

Luke's Gospel tells the Nativity story of the baby in the manger

That night, angels appeared to shepherds on the nearby hills. They said that God's messiah had been born – the Christ. The shepherds went to the town and found Jesus.

One of the best-known stories of the whole Bible is in Luke. It is a story Jesus told when he was a preacher: the parable of the Good Samaritan. In the story, a man is robbed and left for dead in the road. A Temple priest hurries by. A Temple helper comes to look but also hurries on by. Then comes a Samaritan – someone who would not have worshipped at the Temple in Jerusalem. But the Samaritan stops to help the man, takes him to an inn and pays for him to be taken care of. Jesus told his listeners to act like the Samaritan, who was kind.

Like all the Gospels, Luke tells how Jesus' enemies had him executed: nailed to a cross of wood. Luke, as always, shows that Jesus was kind and merciful. From the cross, Luke writes, Jesus said this: 'Forgive them, Father! They don't know what they are doing.'

Inn

Wounded man

Samaritan

17 John and the Story of Jesus

WHO WAS JOHN?

An ancient tradition says that John's Gospel was written by the same fisherman who was one of Jesus' first disciples.

This Gospel says that, as Jesus hung on the cross, he saw his mother with John and asked him to take care of her.

The Last Supper in Matthew, Mark and Luke

Jesus shares the bread

Jesus shares the cup of wine

The Gospel of **John** is different from the other Gospels: more of it is the words that Jesus preached and less of it is story. There is one place where Jesus describes himself as the good shepherd. Just as a real shepherd will protect his creatures from wild animals, so Jesus wants to keep his followers safe. He will even die for them.

One very important story about Jesus tells of the last supper he shared with his disciples. In **Matthew**, **Mark** and **Luke**, it is the Passover meal. This remembered the old covenant. Jesus made a new promise – a new covenant.

'Jesus took a piece of bread, gave thanks to God, broke it, and gave it to his disciples, saying, "This is my body, which is given for you. Do this in memory of me."

'In the same way he gave them the cup of wine after the supper, saying, "This cup is God's new covenant sealed with my blood, which is poured out for you."'

Jesus' followers believe that these words came true the next day. Jesus was crucified – his body broken and his blood spilt. Three days later he rose to life. It promised that those who believed in him would have everlasting life: they would be God's people for ever.

The Last Supper in the Gospel of John

A disciple is surprised to be waited on

Jesus does a servant's job

John tells a different story. Before the meal, Jesus washed his disciples' dusty feet. He told them to act in the same kind of way and be servants of one another. Then he gave them a new commandment: 'Love one another. As I have loved you, so you must love one another.'

John's Gospel says that from the cross Jesus asked John to take care of his mother, Mary

18 The First Christians

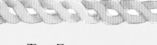

THE EYEWITNESS

*Paul chose companions
to go with him on
his journeys. At some
point, Luke became one
of those companions.
Luke writes about what
happened as someone
who was there and saw
it: an eyewitness.*

Pentecost fire

Disciples

The four Gospels all describe one amazing event: after Jesus was crucified and buried, he rose again. His friends and followers saw him alive. Jesus told them to go on doing the work he had begun. He wanted them to spread the message about God's kingdom.

The Gospel writer Luke wrote a second book about what Jesus' followers did next. It is called the **Acts of the Apostles**. An apostle is someone who is sent to do something; this book is about the deeds of those whom Jesus sent to preach his message.

Jesus said a final goodbye and was taken up to heaven. His followers continued to meet together, waiting for a sign Jesus had promised that they should begin their mission. On the day of the harvest festival, Pentecost, that sign came. Luke's account says they heard a noise like rushing wind and saw flames leaping above their heads: God's Holy Spirit came and gave them wisdom and confidence.

From that day on they began to preach. The people who had not trusted Jesus were surprised and angry. In spite of all the dangers, Jesus' followers preached boldly and many people were eager to become followers too. Among the people who tried to silence them was an eager young rabbi named Saul. Even as he was on his way to arrest some of the new believers, he saw a blinding light. He believed he heard Jesus speaking to him. These things made Saul change his mind. He came to believe that Jesus really was the messiah, the Christ. He became a Christian.

Saul was eager to help spread the news about Jesus. He became better known by the Roman form of his name – Paul – and travelled to many places in the Roman empire.

Soon there were groups of Christians in many places in the empire. These were the young churches.

Harbour

Grain ship

Paul travels far and wide to tell people about Jesus

19 Letters to Christians

PAUL'S LETTERS TO FRIENDS

Some of Paul's letters were to churches. Others were to individuals.

1 and 2 Timothy were letters to a young man of that name who was a church leader and a friend and companion of Paul.

Titus was to another helper, who became a leader of the church in Crete.

Philemon was a member of the church in Colossae. Paul wrote this letter asking Philemon to welcome the messenger: he was Onesimus, his former slave, who had run away and then become a Christian.

Wherever the apostles went preaching, they gathered more and more people who wanted to follow Jesus. These people began meeting in their communities. Each group was called a church.

These new believers had never met Jesus in his lifetime on earth. They needed to learn about their new faith. How much of it was about keeping to the laws that Jesus himself had treasured – the laws of the old covenant? Had Jesus changed things?

Paul tells the Thessalonians to keep working and not just wait for Jesus to come again

Thessalon

Rome

In his letter to the Romans Paul sends greetings to his old friends Priscilla and Aquila

Corinth

Paul's letters to the Corinthians reminds them that love is the most important thing of all

What did it mean to be part of God's kingdom? Those people who understood the faith better wrote letters to churches to help answer their questions. These writings were treasured. They were read aloud at meetings and sometimes copies were sent to other churches so they could read them too. In time some of these were considered to be so important that they became part of the Bible.

Paul's friends in Philippi include the wealthy Lydia and the town jailor

Philippi

Region of Galatia

Ephesus

Colossae

Paul explains to the Galatians how both Jews and non-Jews can be Christians

One of the messengers that brings Paul's letter to the Colossians is the runaway slave Onesimus

Paul tells the Ephesians that parents and children must love and respect each other

20 Gathering the Books

REVELATION

*The last book in the Christian Bible is called **Revelation**. The writer names himself as John and says he is describing visions. His book talks of angels and demons and a great battle between good and evil. It ends with a glimpse of a heavenly city with gates of pearl.*

An angel inspires John to write his message

John, the writer of Revelation

The Jewish people had treasured their writings through hundreds of years. After the work done in the time of **Ezra**, a particular collection of books seemed very important.

In the time of the Greek empire, some Jewish scholars agreed to translate this collection into Greek so Jews anywhere could understand it. The translation became known as the Septuagint. This same collection of books was the Jewish Bible in the time of Jesus.

After Jesus' lifetime, his followers wrote Gospels and letters and accounts of the life of the church. By 150 CE, many of these were being studied eagerly by the believers in their churches. However, there were arguments about which ones could be trusted and which ones could not.

The church leaders asked Christians all over the world to choose. The discussion went backwards and forwards for many years. In 397 CE, at a meeting in Carthage on the coast of Africa, a final list of books was agreed.

The books in the Septuagint became the first part of the Christian Bible: the Old Testament.

The Christian writings became the second part of the Christian Bible: the New Testament.

The official collection is sometimes referred to as the 'canon of scripture'.

Over the centuries, Christians have made translations of their scriptures so that people from different places can read and understand them. In fact, more than 2,000 years have passed since the time of Jesus, and it just so happens that the Bible has been translated into more than 2,000 languages.

Many of the early churches meet in the homes of wealthy Romans who have become Christians

THE DEUTEROCANON

The Old Testament that Christians first chose was all of the writings in the Septuagint. But the Jewish teachers later took another look at their scriptures and decided that a few of the pieces in it were not worth including in their Bible. Some Christian Bibles today have the longer selection, and some the shorter. The extra books are called the Deuterocanon or the Apocrypha.

Index

1

1 Chronicles 8
1 Corinthians 19
1 John 19
1 Kings 8
1 Peter 19
1 Samuel 6, 8
1 Thessalonians 19
1 Timothy 19

2

2 Chronicles 8
2 Corinthians 19
2 John 19
2 Kings 8
2 Peter 19
2 Samuel 8
2 Thessalonians 19
2 Timothy 19

3

3 John 19

A

Abraham 3
Acts of the Apostles 18
Adam 1
Ahab 8
Alexander the Great 13
Amos 8
Andrew 14
Apocrypha 20
apostle, apostles 18, 19
ark of the covenant 5, 7, 9
ascension 18
Assyria, Assyrians 8, 9, 12

B

Babylon, Babylonians 9, 10, 11, 12
Babylonia 3
baptism 13
Barnabas 14
Benjamin 4

Bethlehem 7, 15, 16

C

Canaan 3, 4, 5, 6
Carthage 20
Christ 13, 16, 18
Christians 18, 20
churches 18, 19
Colossae 19
Colossians 19
commandment (new) 17
Corinth 19
covenant 5, 17, 19
crucifixion 14, 16, 17, 18

D

Daniel 10, 11
David 7, 13, 15
Deuterocanon 20
Deuteronomy 5
disciples 14

E

Edomites 9
Egypt 4, 5, 9
Elijah 8
Elisha 8
Ephesians 19
Ephesus 19
Esther 11
Eve 1
Exodus 5
Ezekiel 10
Ezra 12, 20

F

flood 2
foreigners from the East 15
frankincense 15

G

Gabriel 16
Galatia 19

Galatians 19
Galilee 14, 16
Genesis 1, 2, 5
Gentiles 16
gold 15
Goliath 7
Good News 14
Good Samaritan 16
Gospel(s) 14, 15, 16, 17, 18
Greek (language) 16, 20
Greeks, Greek empire 13, 20

H

Habakkuk 9
Haggai 12
Haman 11
Hebrew (language) 3
Hebrews 19
Herod 13
Hezekiah 9
Holy Spirit 13, 18
Hosea 8

I

Isaac 3
Isaiah 9, 10
Israel (country) 1, 8, 9
Israel (people) 6, 7
Israel (person) 3
Israelites 4, 5

J

Jacob 3, 4
James (book) 19
James (disciple) 14
Jeremiah 9
Jericho 6
Jeroboam 8
Jerusalem 7, 8, 9, 12, 13, 16
Jesus 1, 13, 14, 15, 16, 17, 18, 19
Jewish people, Jews 1, 10, 11, 12, 13, 15, 20
Jewish scriptures 12, 15
Jezebel 8